TANA HOBAN

I Read Signs

Greenwillow
Books
New York

This one
is for
all my
children

With many thanks
to all the sign-finders

I Read Signs
Copyright © 1983 by Tana Hoban
All rights reserved.
Manufactured in China
www.harperchildrens.com
First Edition
17 16 15 14 13 12 11

Library of Congress
Cataloging in Publication Data

Hoban, Tana.
I read signs.
"Greenwillow Books."
Summary: Introduces signs
and symbols frequently
seen along the street.
1. Traffic signs and signals
—Juvenile literature.
2. Street signs—
Juvenile literature.
3. Signs and signboards—
Juvenile literature.
[1. Traffic signs and signals.
2. Street signs.
3. Signs and signboards.
4. Signs and symbols]
I. Title.
TE228.H63 1983
001.55'2   83-1482
ISBN 0-688-02317-7 (trade)
ISBN 0-688-02318-5 (lib. bdg.)
ISBN 0-688-07331-X (pbk.)

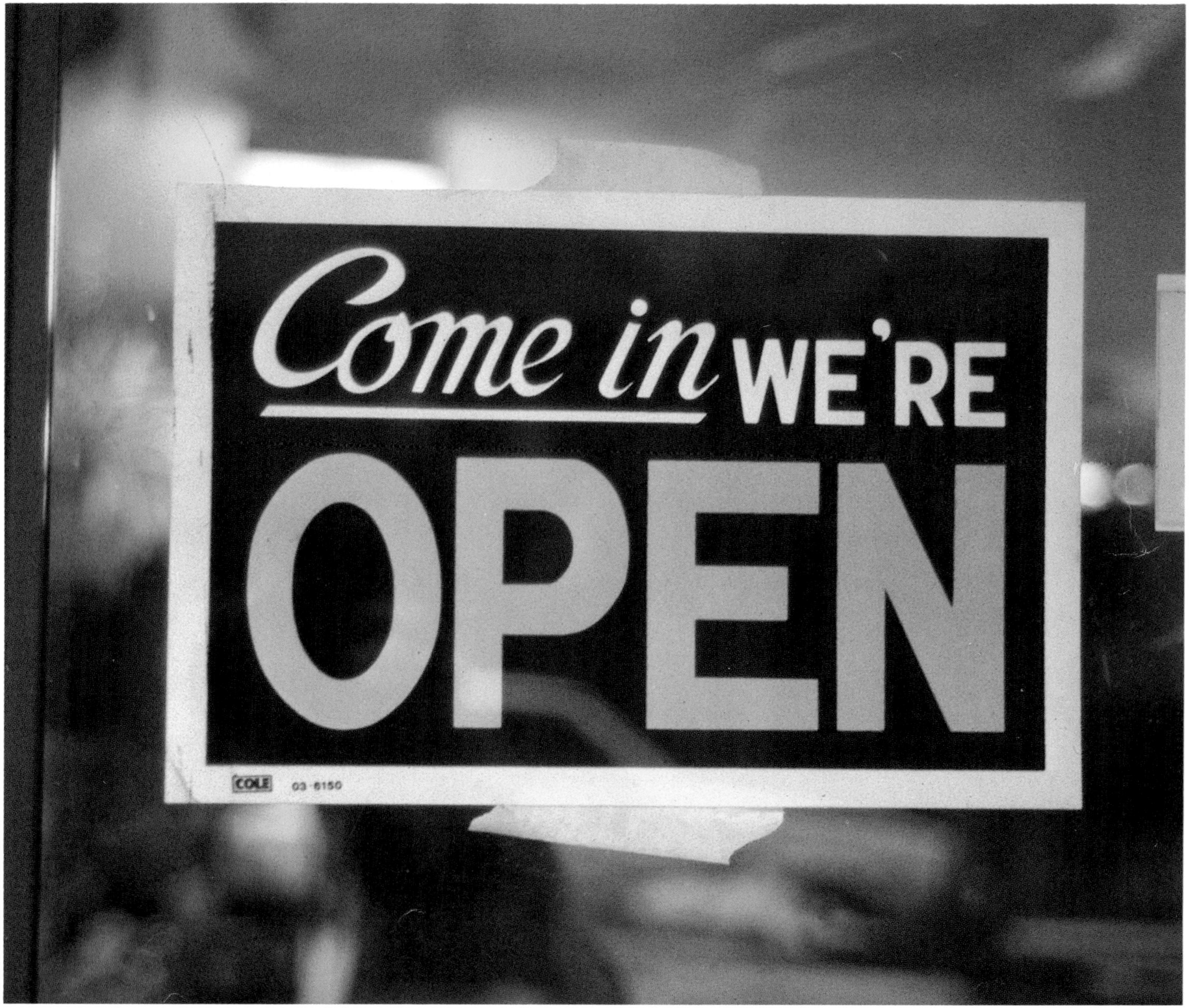
Come in WE'RE
OPEN
COLE 03-6150

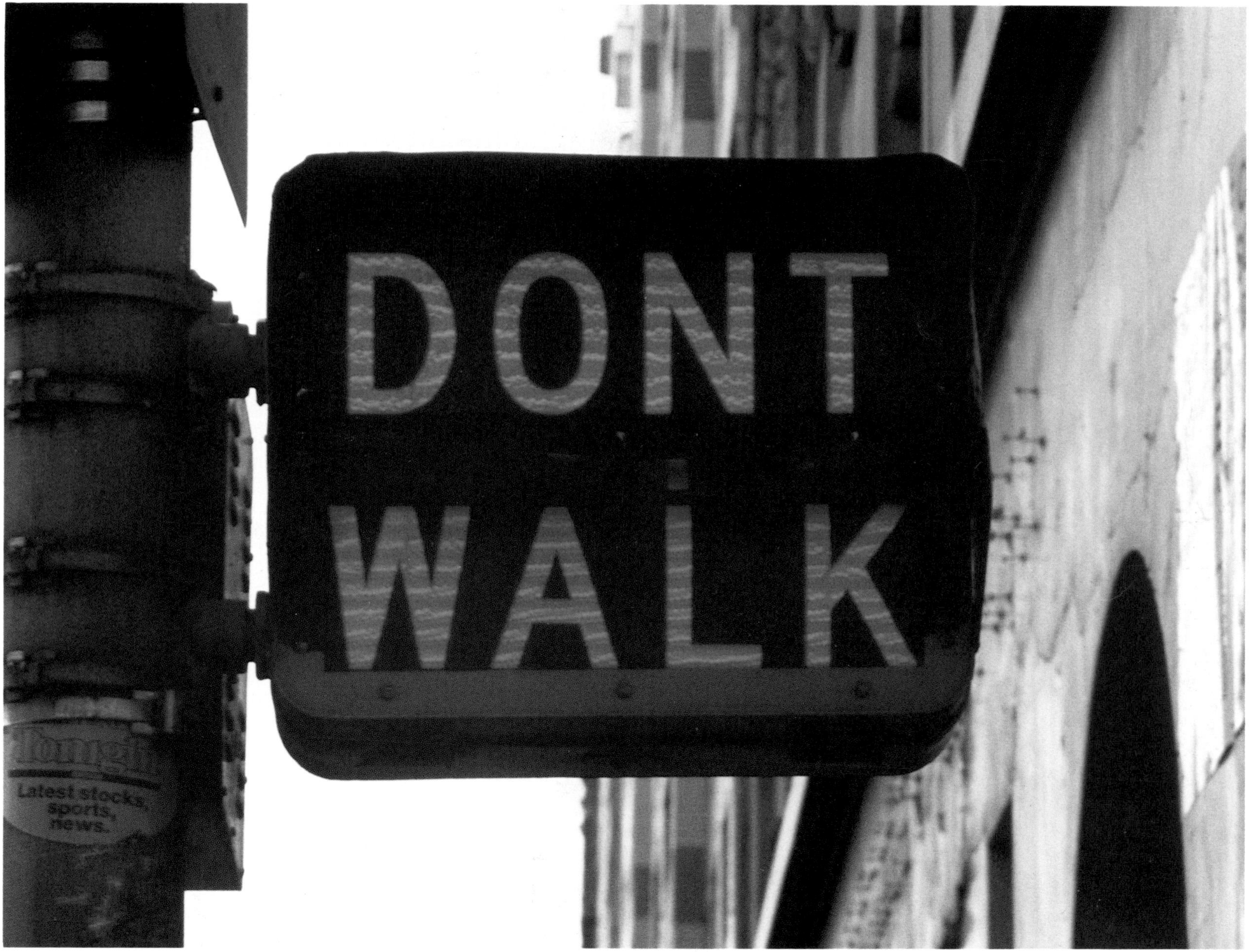
DONT
WALK
Latest stocks,
sports,
news.

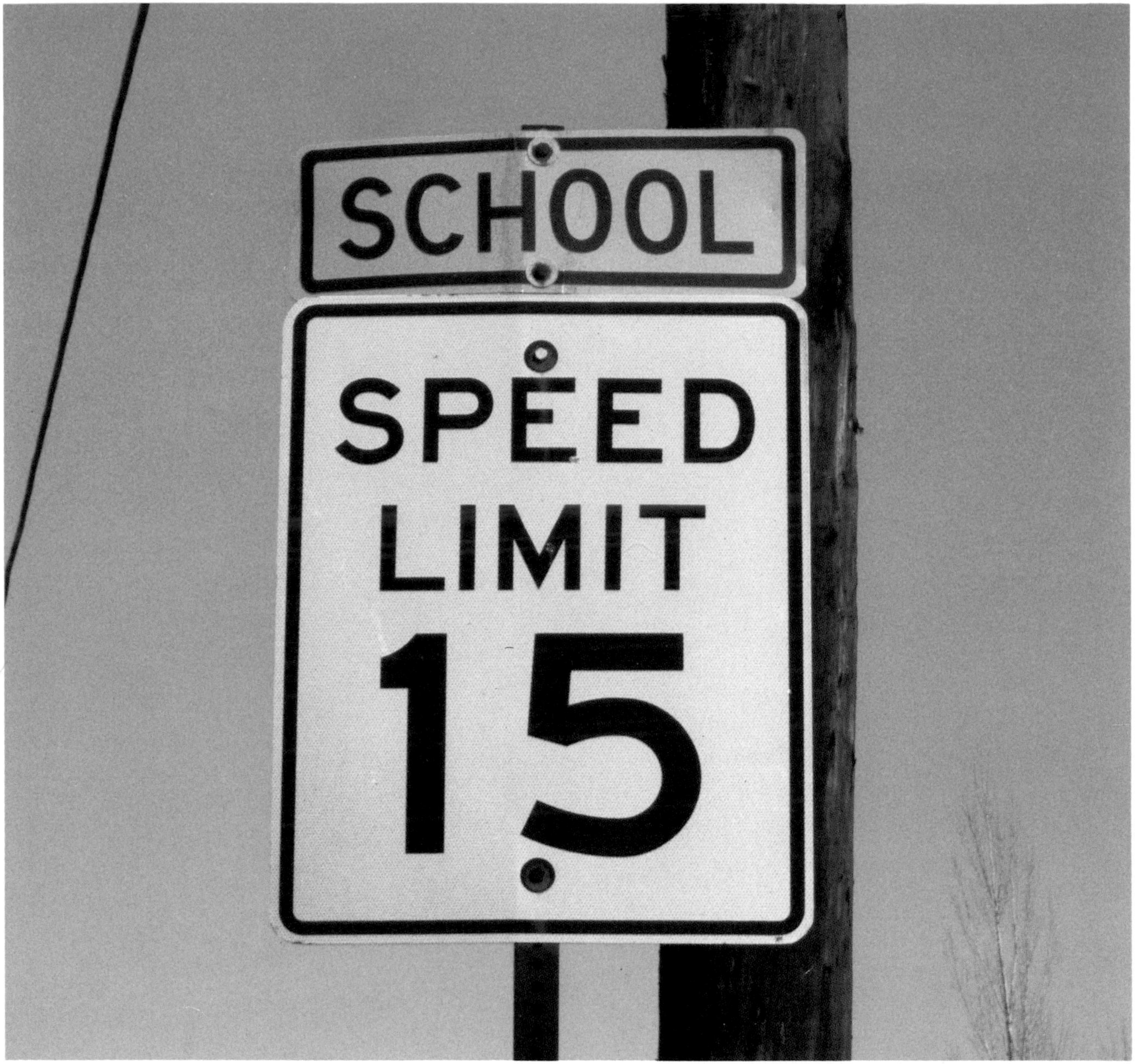
SCHOOL
SPEED
LIMIT
15

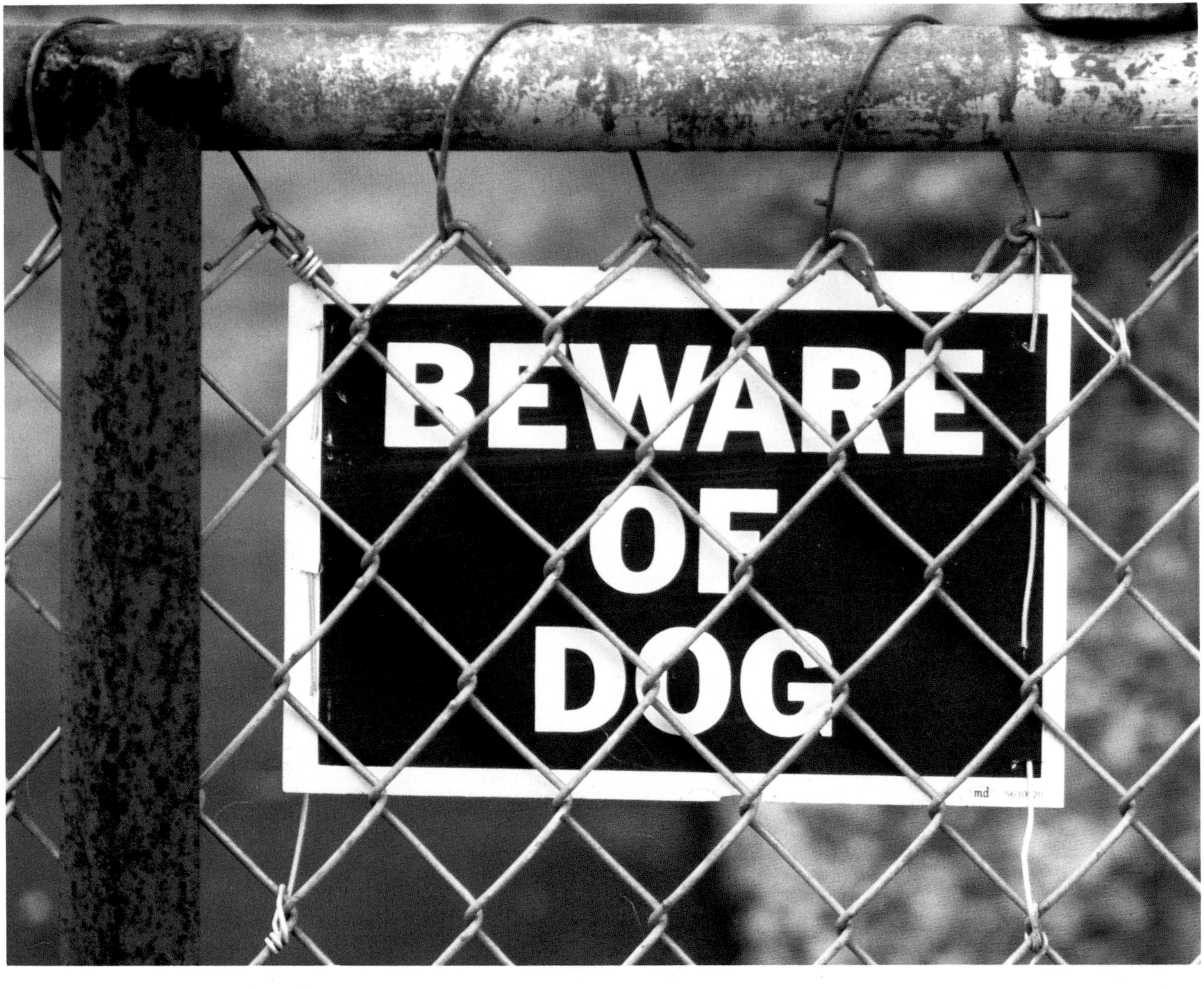
BEWARE
OF
DOG

← FIRE HOSE

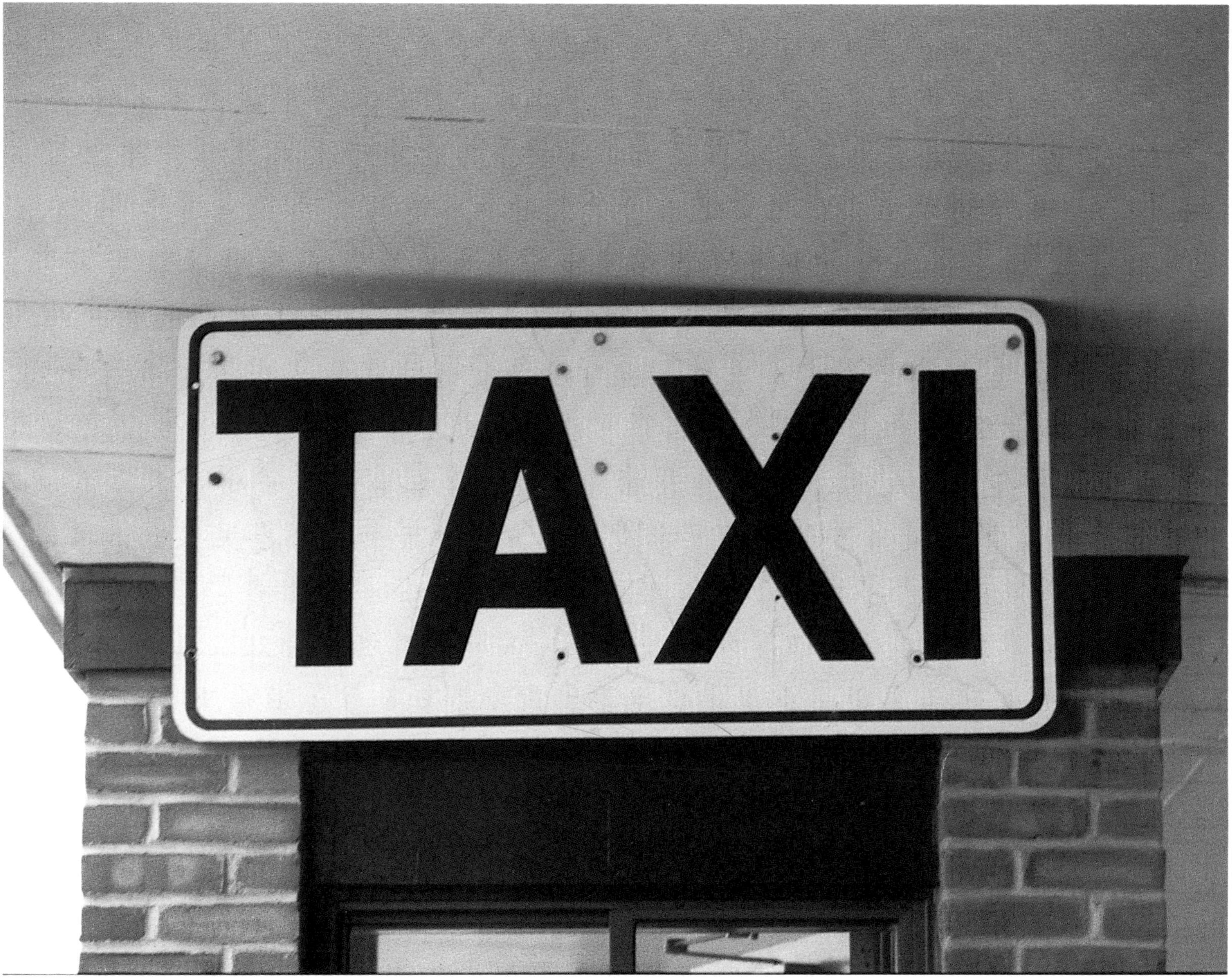
TAXI

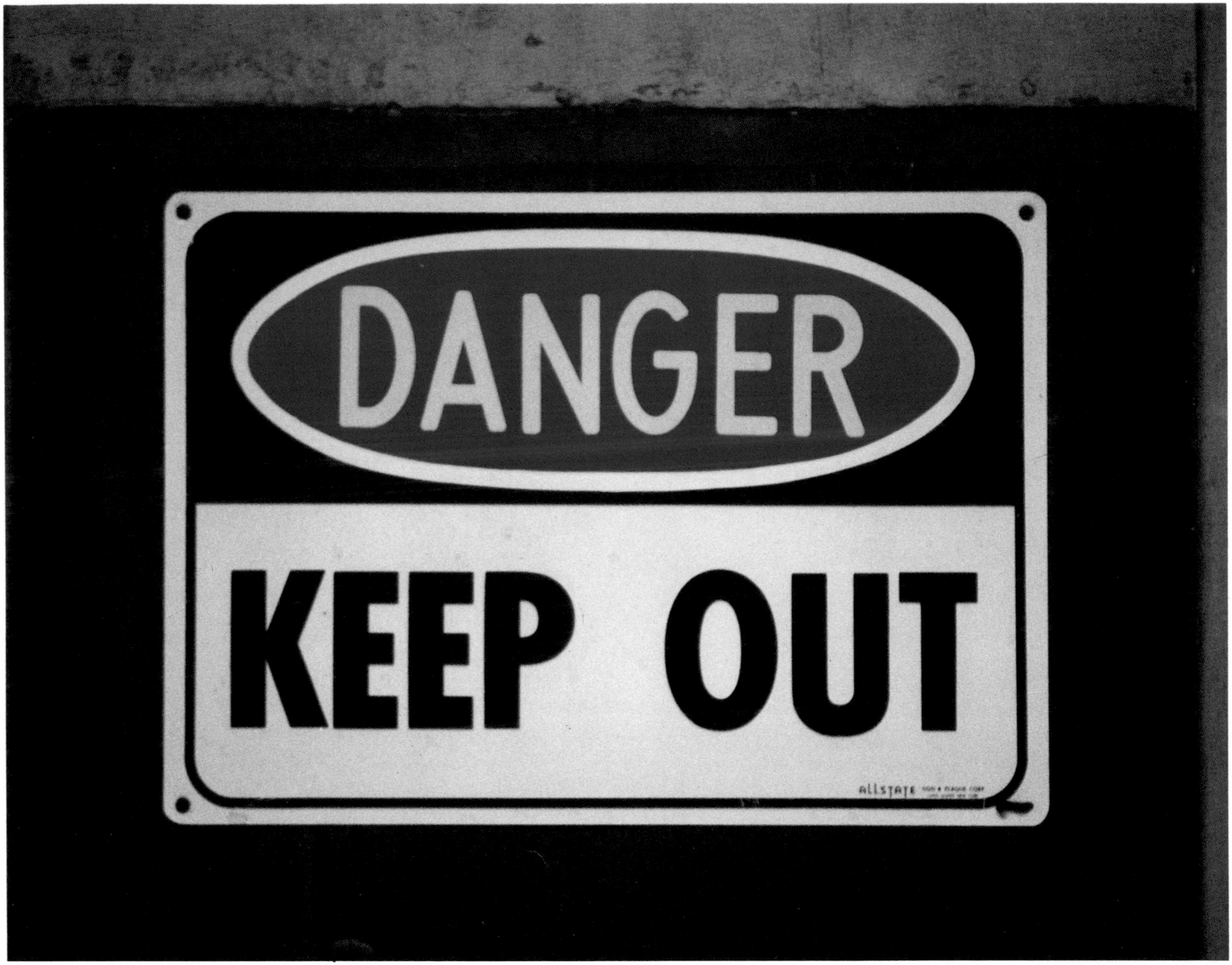
DANGER
KEEP OUT
ALLSTATE

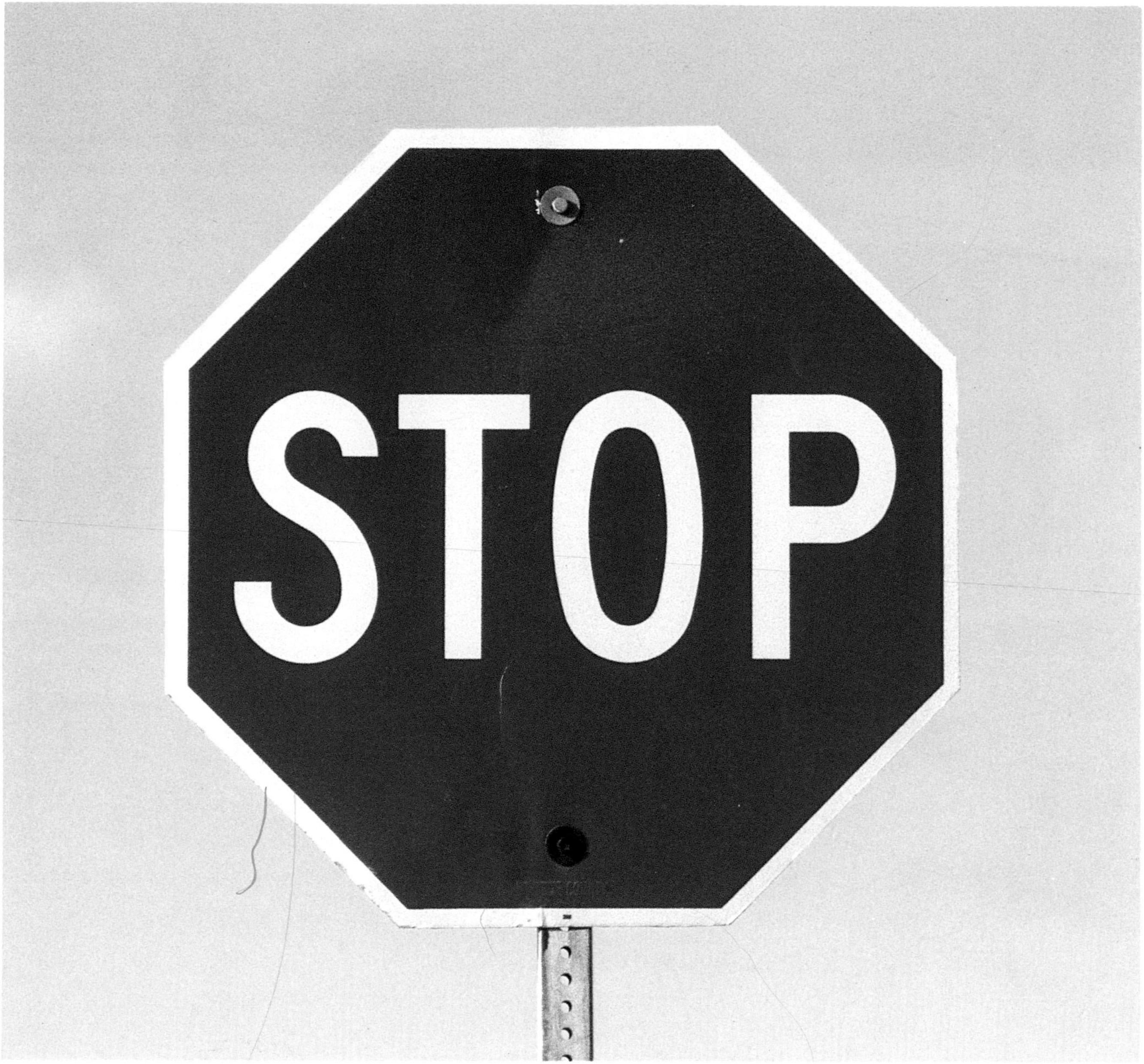
STOP

NO LEFT
TURN

MON THRU FRI

7 AM — 7 PM
MON THRU FRI

TRAFFIC

KEEP

→

RIGHT

DEPT OF TRAFFIC

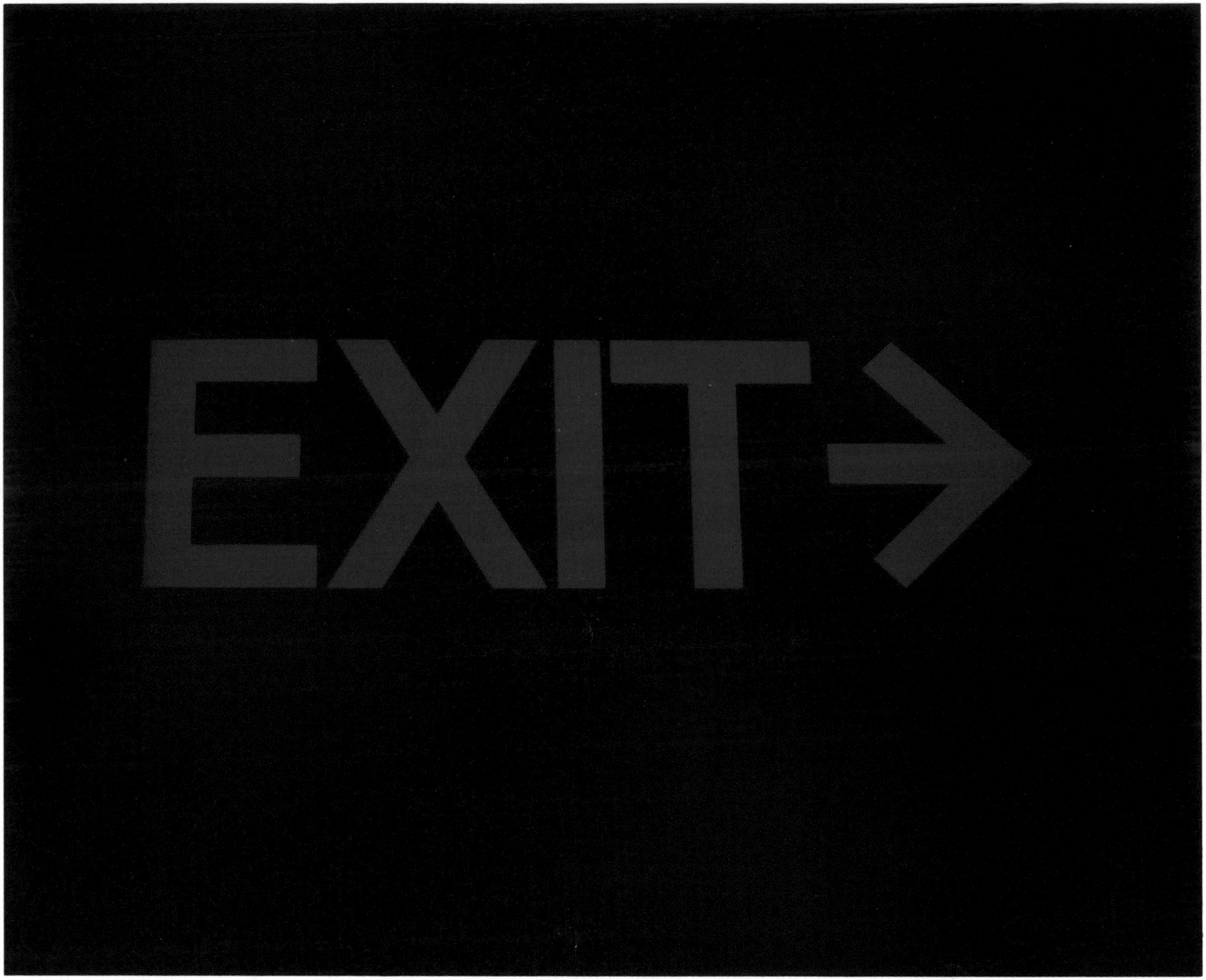
EXIT →

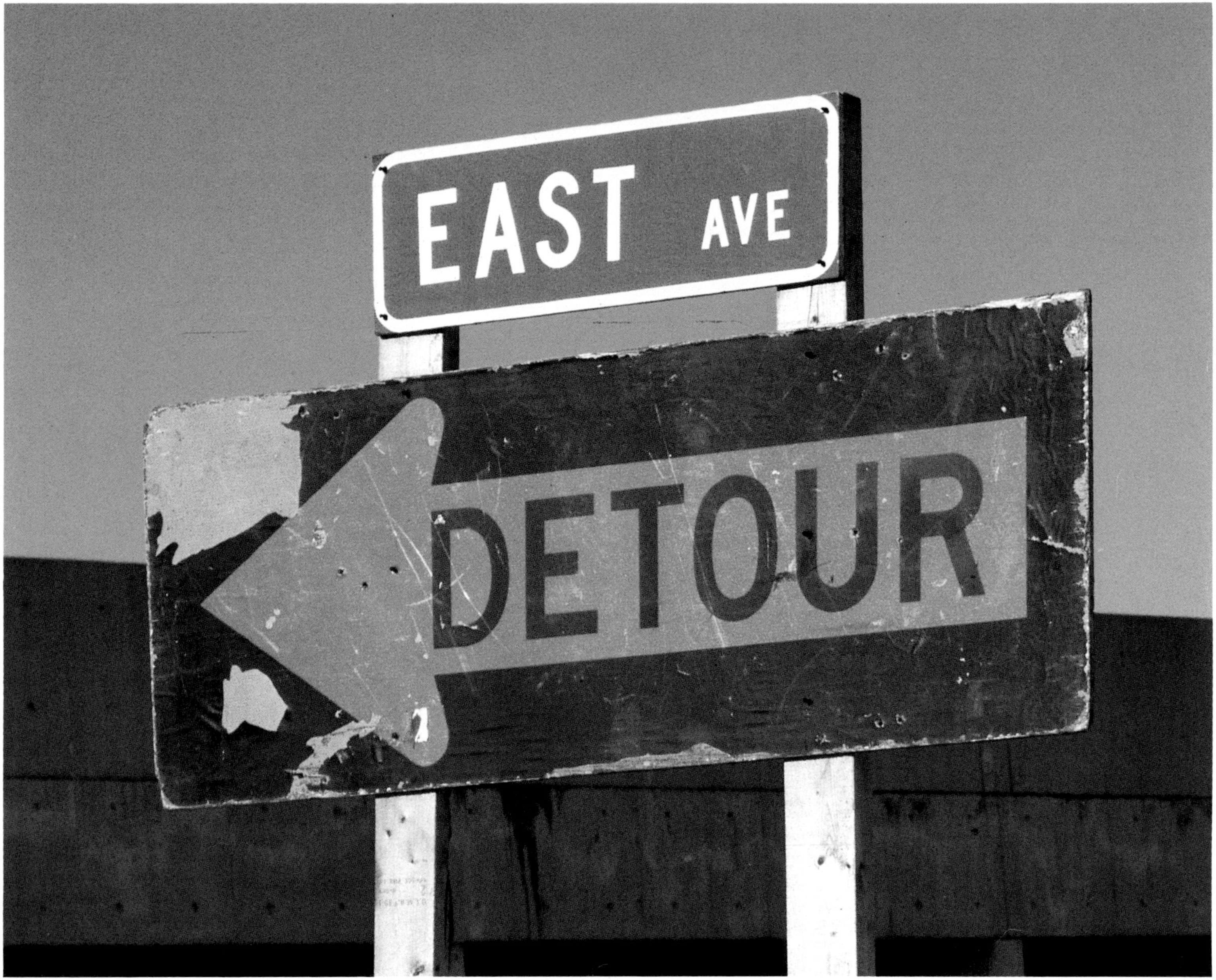
EAST AVE
DETOUR

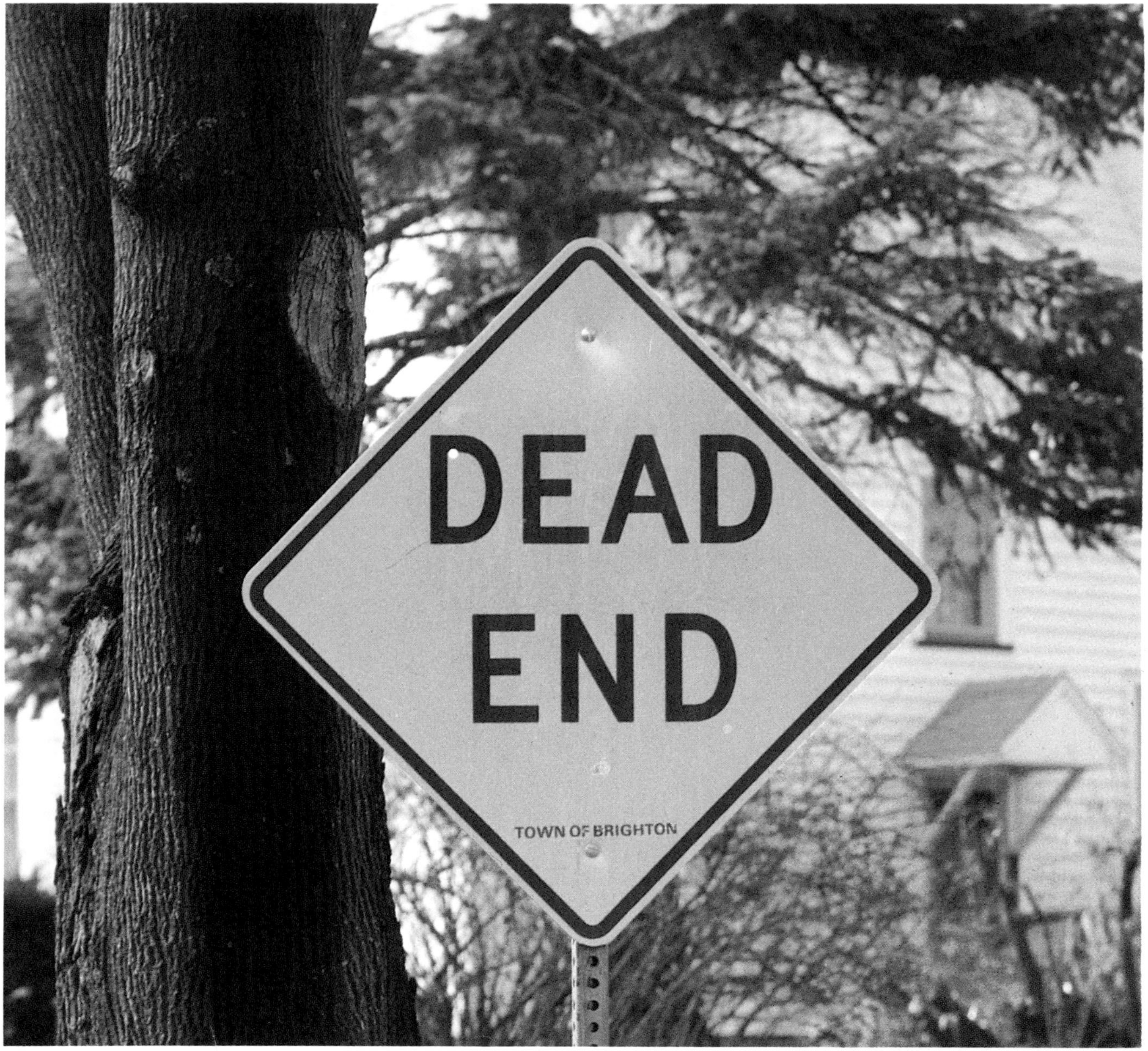
DEAD
END
TOWN OF BRIGHTON

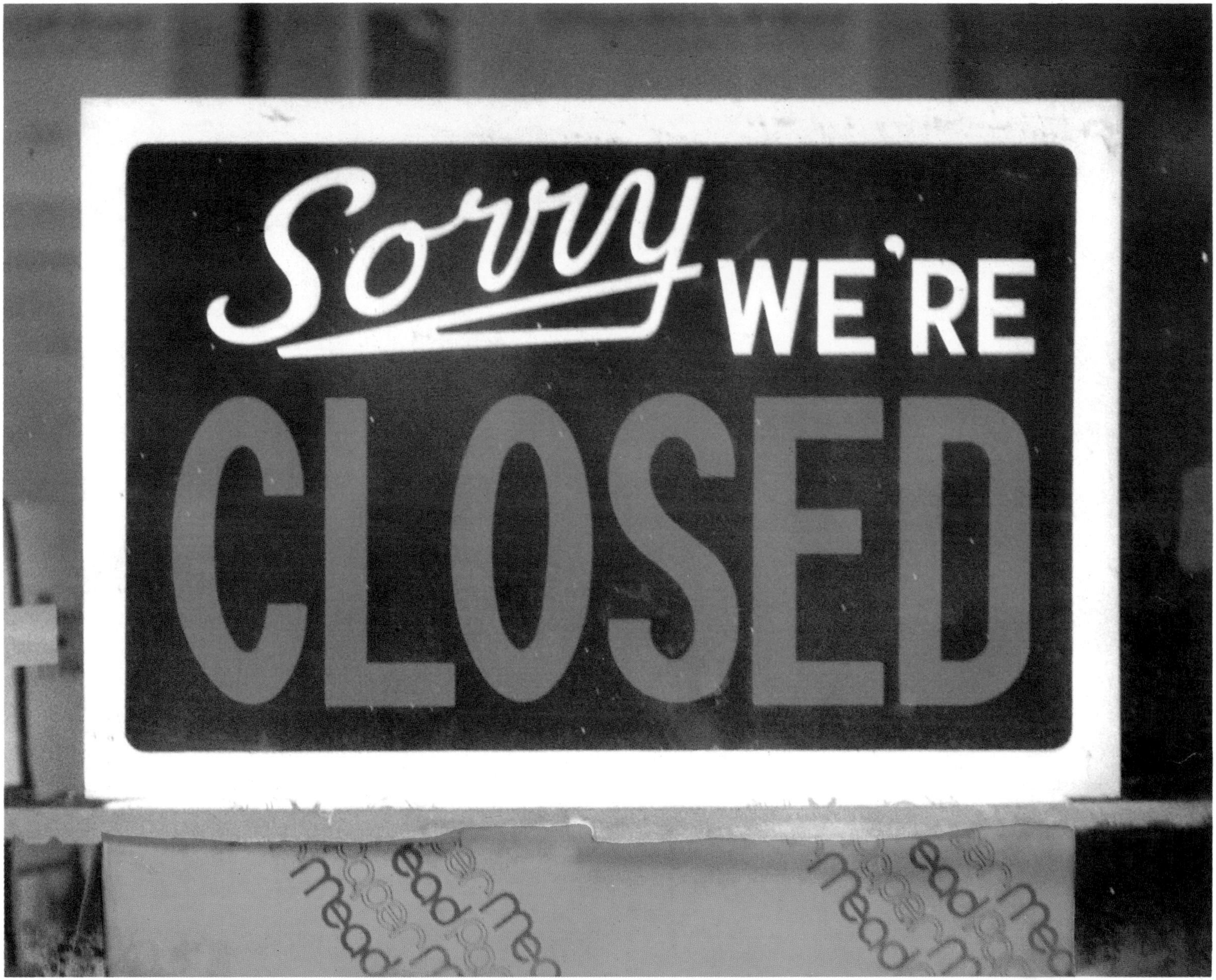
Sorry WE'RE
CLOSED